HOW TO HANDLE A MAJOR CRISIS

Peter J Daniels

THE HOUSE OF TABOR

OTHER TITLES BY PETER J. DANIELS
How To Be Happy Though Rich
How To Reach Your Life Goals
How To Be Motivated All The Time
How To Have The Awesome Power of Public Speaking
Miss Phillips You Were Wrong

Tutorial programs:
Destiny
How To Get More Done And Have Time Left Over

All correspondence to:
World Centre for Entrepreneurial Studies
38–40 Carrington Street, Adelaide, South Australia 5000
Telephone: (08) 231 0111 Facsimile: (08) 211 8423

How To Handle A Major Crisis
Copyright © 1987 by Peter J. Daniels
National Library of Australia card number
and ISBN 0 949330 21 3

The author would like to thank Peter Haran for his valued assistance in the writing of this book.

Printed by Australian Print Group,
P.O. Box 81, Sassafras, Victoria 3787,
Australia.

Published by **The House of Tabor**
84 Northgate Street,
Unley Park, South Australia 5061.

Dedicated to my friend
Dr. Robert H. Schuller,
who has faced and successfully
overcome more crises
than any man I know

When our strong optimistic desire
to think, commit and work
exceeds by far
our weak, negative fear of failure,
then success is always
guaranteed

Contents

Preface

It usually starts with a phone call. . . 'You don't know me, but. . .' and then the whole sad, sorry story spills out.

The creditors are closing in. . . the business is on the skids. . . the money has run out. . . we have our backs to the wall. Sometimes the calls are emotional, often angry, but usually cries for help in a seemingly hopeless situation.

Most of us encounter problems from time to time and usually we cope with them or they disappear of their own accord leaving us older and wiser.

For example, the loss of a loved one is a crisis that often leaves a permanent scar. The same with a critical medical problem in our lives or the lives of those close to us.

The purpose of this book is to help those with major financial crises. But I hope the principles presented here will provide help in other areas of life as well.

Peter J. Daniels

Time To Dream

It seems it's time to dream again,
Dream wide and very high.

It seems it's time to dream again,
To be great before I die.

It seems it's time to dream again,
Of enterprises vast.

It seems it's time to dream again,
Of something that will last.

It seems it's time to dream again,
And accept God's sovereign will.

It seems it's time to dream again,
And move from being still.

It seems it's time to dream again,
And build my life anew.

It seems it's time to dream again,
Yes, it's time for me and you.

Peter J. Daniels

CHAPTER ONE

Remove the Imagery

Your attitude in any major crisis is the first thing over which you can take control. It is through personal control that you obtain reassurance and stability.

CHAPTER ONE

Remove the Imagery

When a major crisis hits, a reaction can form in many different ways. It may be a cold feeling deep in the stomach followed by despair. At other times it may be panic followed by fear or calmness, or guilt.

But there is one thing for sure — there will be a reaction depending on the size of the calamity and the direct relationship it has upon your family, yourself and your livelihood.

The most important factor in any crisis is to *take control at inception*, realising that through control you remain captain of the ship, guiding it out of troubled waters.

The key control factor in a crisis is your *attitude*. It is more important than circumstances and is the most positive — or negative — factor in any crisis.

Your attitude is more relevant than facts, more versatile than circumstances, more powerful than opposition, more resilient than pressure and more

flexible than time. It is more valuable than money
or influence and far more forceful than markets.

Your attitude in any major crisis is the first thing
over which you can take control. Through personal control you obtain reassurance and stability.

You must firstly deal with *emotions*. When a
major crisis strikes, images of catastrophe come
wildly into play. Your mind is filled with pictures
and thoughts of both possibilities and impossibil-
ities.

Do not expect the imagination to follow any
pattern, and do not be alarmed at the enormity
and range of disasters it portrays. But do accept it
for what it is — a warning signal flashing images to
grab your attention and ready you for battle.

I remember going broke many years ago and
the shame I felt because I had let my family down
both as a father and a husband. I had not lived up
to what I thought I should have been. My imagination was focused on cheques I had sent out in
good faith which were now being dishonoured. I
was without a job or any source of income.

I had visions of my home being taken away and
even contemplated going to jail over bad debts. I
suddenly felt everyone was watching me and no
one would ever trust me again. I could not sleep,
eat or think straight and the images of the worst
possible kind were my constant companions.
They burned up energy and produced nothing.

I decided then and there to commit my fears to

paper, however crazy they seemed to be. I also needed to get the facts down on paper — in an opposing column — in an effort to remove the negative imagery. At the very least, I had to understand the reality of the situation, and I responded in the following way:

Firstly, I would take control of my attitude. In effect, I would try to act like the type of person I could admire under adverse conditions. I would think with positive reality and consistently present a cheerful disposition. I would let no one direct me away from that first principal.

Secondly, I would write down in detail all the worst known facts and fears on paper in an exaggerated form, either positive or negative.

Thirdly, I would translate all those facts and fears into costs, goods, and reputations to provide a clear picture of what I was faced with.

Fourthly, I would turn all that documentation into a 'time sheet of disaster' emanating from the major crisis.

Fifthly, I would accept total responsibility for the crisis and all the repercussions.

Sixthly, I would write all the facts, fears and the timesheet along with my affirmation of responsibility on to a large piece of cardboard and place it where I could see it.

This done I would prevent my mind from wandering and keep my mind on the facts. I also could update the chart as circumstances changed (they always do in a crisis).

The result of this initiative was *I removed the fanciful imagery* because I had the facts and a formula for monitoring progress. My energies were now channeled in a positive direction.

CRISIS CONTROL
- Take control of your attitude.
- Accept total responsibility.
- Get the facts documented.

Beat The Mood

There is a 'mood' around today that dulls the mind
  and spirit,
It fools the heart and kills the will and makes you feel
  'not with it'.
Have you been duped into being less than you really
  ought to be?
Then learn the way to overcome 'the mood'
  convincingly.

A heavy cloud of doom and gloom directs the
  hopeless course,
The road of doubt and tragedy runs downhill from
  this source;
But darkness can be sent to flight with good thoughts
  tried and true.
With dreams fulfilled by action and performance
  carried through.

You can cross the toughest valley, any mountain you
  can climb,
And obstacles you'll overcome with persistence and
  with time.
In the end you burst right through because your
  spirit is within;
You know deep in your heart of hearts you really
  want to win.

And then towards life's journey's end, approaching
  sunset time,
You look up glad to recognise the Master's beckon-
  ing sign.
You beat the mood! You did perform! The race of life
  you won!
And now you stand with heroes and your destiny
  has come!
Well done, you beat 'the mood'!

Peter J. Daniels

Role Playing And Past Victories

I decided if I accepted myself as a full person with some obvious flaws that could be dealt with, then I could overcome, benefit from and be better for the experience.

Role Playing And Past Victories

Everybody has encountered difficulties, and probably most of them were self-inflicted.

I recall speaking once with a friend's brother and I remarked about the number of difficulties my friend had overcome. His brother responded: 'Yes, he has always been that way. As a matter of fact, if he didn't have a problem he would create one!'

You've probably heard that statement before, and it is a truism — many people move from crisis to crisis throughout their lives, burning up energy and minimising their effectiveness. While it certainly is true everyone has problems, difficulties and crises from time to time, it is also true that *everyone has victories as well.*

With the fear and isolation of failure pressing down upon you it is sometimes difficult to recall times of victory and exhilaration.

During one of the deep financial crises in my

life, when all looked black and there was little hope, I walked along the beach to try and gain some sanity and clarity of thought from the rhythm of the sea. As I walked I reflected on more joyous times and tried to relive past victories. I had nothing to look forward to except creditors' meetings, criticism and defeat! But I was convinced there had to be a way to get through all that and still come out the other side a whole person with self respect intact. Surely additional lessons could also be learnt.

Well, the lesson I learnt that day was life-changing and I share it with all I meet facing a major crisis. It has its roots deep within the biblical charge 'whatever things are of good report, think on these things,' (Philippians 4:6-7).

My action on returning home that night was to create a *Victory Book.* I would go back over my life and document all the things I could remember doing well. When I felt down or disappointed, I would pull out that book and read aloud all of God's goodness in my life. I would be a shouting optimist within the hour!

I put this Victory Book into some kind of sequence, collating similar experiences together and putting behind me all the hurtful events from the past. I accepted them only as learning tools, resharpened to get the job of life done well.

I came to understand afresh that if I allowed my mind to focus on my future destruction through any crisis, I was, in a sense, hating myself and burning up energy along with self-worth. I decided that if I accepted myself as a full person with some obvious flaws that could be dealt with, then I could overcome, benefit from and be better for the experience.

Sometimes under great pressure I would lounge in a chair for hours reliving past experiences, like the times when I worked for a timber firm, and was told it was impossible to sell hardboard on the West Coast of South Australia against our competitors.

I recall pleading with my sales manager to allow me to go into the area they called 'the salesman's graveyard' — so-called because of the enormous distances that had to be covered over bad roads for such a small market.

I suggested because of those reasons it was probably never serviced properly and I was convinced of a veritable bonanza. Because I had an excellent track record — and offered to do the trip during my vacation — the sales manager relented, although he was quite concerned about the expense.

The result was I sold more in two weeks than had previously been sold in the whole year. In addition, I saw two large hardboard mills put on a 24-hour-a-day shift to keep up with the sales. I received a Super Genius Award for excellence.

Such were my role playing sessions, comprising several victories a session. I also re-read past letters of congratulations with photographs of earlier successful events and this all helped to tip the scales during my crisis, creating a positive environment.

Why don't you develop your own Victory Book, based not so much on how others saw the events, but rather how you saw them, and were affected by them?

In so doing you resavor some of the flavor from past conquests, and can count on being uplifted and inspired.

I also make a point of reading biographies to help retain the optimism and objectivity. We must realise that only those who face crises, overcome and endure are those who develop character and experience to press on to higher things. In years to come you are going to look back at your major crisis and recognise it for what it was — a test in which you had to qualify.

Recognise too, that we will always deal with the same base material: ourselves.

CRISIS CONTROL
- Accept that everybody has difficulties and victories.
- By reflecting on victories you can gain strength for the future.
- Create your own Victory Book.

CHAPTER THREE

Put The Threat Into Perspective

Because most major crises have a finality about them, we tend to feel that unless we overcome, all will be lost. Thankfully, this is not the case.

CHAPTER THREE

Put The Threat Into Perspective

Whenever we are faced with a major crisis we are immediately put under pressure. All problems become distorted and magnified.

The easiest way to intimidate another person is to put him under threat because a threat is full of unknowns, peppered with enough fact to make it believable and frightening. The power of a threat of impending disaster due to a financial or other crisis lies in us accepting the unknowns. Once of course, the threat has been carried out, the fear has been satisfied and it's back to business as usual, or near as usual as possible under changed circumstances.

A threat perceived is usually worse than a threat performed and possibly the most fearful part of any threat in a major crisis is how much *ego damage we can take.*

I was forced to come to grips with ego damage many years ago when I realised nothing is quite as

final as we might think and what seems to be
impossible to handle today can become a routine
matter once the acceptance level has been
reached.

It occurred after a minor operation when I found
I had an infection and my doctor hesitantly
informed me that two-thirds of my hair was going
to fall out! The doctor was aware of my television
appearances and speaking engagements — not
to mention my continual visibility at work and
other public functions.

My first response was 'Will it grow back again?'

'Yes,' he assured me, 'but it will take several
months.' Then he added, 'It will begin to fall out in a
week.'

There was relief and I laughed and told him I
had been through much worse than that. I could
easily handle the ego damage. He was a little
stunned and reminded me of my public engagements, the looks I would get from people.

The immediate problem was that I was hosting
overseas guests on a speaking and singing tour
throughout Australia. During the week I would be
in the spotlight as I introduced them.

The bottom line was I did lose two-thirds of my
hair and I had to paint my head with brown paint
every morning for months and then spread my
hair around to get maximum coverage! But I
survived and life went on.

The crisis in our life is *always relative*. Think

about it. On a score of one to 10 what would you consider horrific? How would you rate losing your family in a car crash or your children admitting they were on drugs? What about facing a jail sentence for life for a crime you didn't commit? Imagine the worst and rate it on a scale up to 10. Now put your major crisis on the same scale. You may find you have a feeling of gratefulness!

Another curious aspect of a major crisis is we often feel we would rather have someone else's misfortune. This is because we believe we could handle it better, and so be better off. We also feel like this because we are in reality divorced from the emotional stress and circumstances of the other individual. *You will notice from that perspective you manage to get the other person's crisis into the right perspective!*

As previously stated, deal with emotions first and clear your mind. Then progress can be made. You already have the right attitude, your confidence is up through role playing and the threat has been dealt with.

The next move in getting the major crisis into perspective is to deal with *time frames*. It may take three months or more to recover from a major crisis.

Consider at this point a basic course in high level management under classroom conditions —we have problems to solve and an examination will take place.

Accept the threat only as probable and if it does happen it may be bigger or smaller than anticipated. But also accept the crisis as a project for growth. Most importantly, now the threat becomes an exciting challenge rather than a fearful burden.

A word of caution at this juncture: remember to pay attention to your personal ethics during a crisis. During this period your mind will perform gymnastics and justify all manner of actions out of character. No crisis is worth losing your integrity — particularly financial integrity — where you are forced to face reality.

Because most major crises have a finality about them, we tend to feel that unless we overcome them all will be lost forever. Thankfully this is not the case. Nothing is final, not even death (if you accept the Christian charter as being true).

The big threat, if we analyse it thoroughly, is in the areas of pride, fear, worry, pain and failure.

And bear in mind that defeat is only a temporary condition. The war is not over until we have totally surrendered. And never allow yourself to hate or blame others. This burns up energy by the ton and kills self-worth, while compassion, patience and understanding restore energy and self-worth.

I have also found in a major crisis — particularly a financial one — that yesterday's friends can become today's enemies, with a good deal of emotional blackmail used against you.

The major financial crisis is the one that sorts out those who play by the rules and those who only use the rules of good conduct and courtesy for convenience.

CRISIS CONTROLS

- Remember — threats are magnified under pressure.
- How do you rate your threat?
- Threats test your ethics as well as those of others.
- Watch your integrity and that of your 'friends'.

Plan A Countdown

Our progress in life is in direct proportion to the size of the crisis, our response to the crisis and the lessons that can be learned from the crisis.

Plan A Countdown

I reiterate that the essence of handling a crisis is to maintain control at all times. I would be the first to admit this is easier said than done, but it can be done provided you have a *planned countdown.*

Step number one is to obtain accurate legal advice as to where you stand. Secondly, examine all documents and make sure — individuals and companies — including the government — are not implying aspects that are irrelevant or incorrect.

You have two very simple options in a major crisis: *let it happen, or make it happen.*

The first choice is still a choice even if the crisis has occurred — you can move to stage two for a follow through, or you can mop up and regain control. If the crisis is impending, or happening, *take charge now.*

At all times ensure you retain your good name and dignity. Do this by actually becoming involved in the winding up. After all you are better equipped than any other to handle it. Right?

The secret is to obtain all information at hand —the limits and calls on you imposed by others and the time frames you have to work within. Now work out a countdown within those time frames and leave no loose ends.

Paste your information down on a big diagram, cross out each item when it is finalised and move straight on to the next. Your chart may need updating from time to time because early evaluation may be incorrect.

While you are preparing this stage you may encounter those in authority who will attempt to place you at their beck and call. A case in point comes to mind here. A friend of mine was almost totally broke during a major financial crisis and was being bullied by a solicitor acting for the creditors. My friend was in such a bewildered state, trying to salvage his business, he was near physical and mental collapse. Adding to his plight was the attitude of the solicitor, who was demanding my friend negotiate for hours over documents and explain transactions — in anything but a cordial manner.

I was told of this and I suggested to my friend that without his co-operation the solicitor was going to get nowhere. So he should phone the solicitor and inform him of times he would be available and for how long. There would be no deviation. The solicitor accepted the terms. End of problem.

Whatever happens, do not burn up all your energy running around trying to pacify everyone. Lay down ground rules. Remain calm and answer everything put to you with honesty and candour.

When you encounter a major crisis, it rarely comes about suddenly, but rather, difficulties gradually get out of hand. In attempting to stop the catastrophe you can wear yourself out and when the crunch comes you are totally exhausted.

As early as possible *get rest and restore stability* before you commit yourself to a countdown. I carry an affirmation card in my wallet at all times on which is clearly written all the things I stand for and what my goals are until my eightieth birthday. I suggest you carry a similar card stating your ethical and conclusive goals during your crisis.

I have been through a number of crises and I know unless I have an affirmation I will stray off the track, worsening the situation.

When my son Graham was in his early twenties he had a major financial crisis. When I asked if I could help, he said 'No, leave me alone, God has something to teach me and I don't want to miss the experience.' Graham also told his wife, 'We are going to be poor for a while — don't get used to it because it's not going to last.' Graham learned, as I have, that our progress in life is in direct proportion to:

(a) *The size of the crisis*
(b) *Your response to the crisis*
(c) *The lessons that can be learned from that crisis.*

You are finally responsible for your own behaviour in any circumstance and the control factor in that circumstance is your behaviour and how you exercise it.

CRISIS CONTROLS

- Control a crisis.
- Plan a countdown.
- Don't wear yourself out.
- Prepare an affirmation.

CHAPTER FIVE

Extend The Deadline

I recall how broke we were many years ago, not knowing where our next meal was coming from; we searched behind our lounge chairs looking for coins and anything that could be sold to give us cash ...

CHAPTER FIVE

Extend The Deadline

By now you should be aware there is no knight in shining armour or kind benefactor who is likely to charge in and pay all your bills, pat you on the head and solve all your problems.

It could be you are in for the long haul and the grind of just existing from day to day. It may not make sense, but you know you must continue because life must go on.

One of the advantages of a crisis is as it moves along you do find people on the fringe who can be quite analytical and helpful. At the other end of the scale are those who relentlessly pursue and accuse. It is these people that you need to tell in clear terms that you will not be intimidated.

Those with whom you are getting on well will understand your predicament. So *keep them informed and ask for help.* Let them know you are not asking your debts be wiped out, but rather you want to work as a team towards a solution for mutual benefit and satisfaction. Never accept you are in a non-negotiating position and keep uppermost in your mind that all major crises have one paramount problem — *time*. If you have enough time, most problems can be thrashed out.

So the first major decision after the initial shock has passed — and you have taken control — is to extend the deadline. The deadline can be extended by a series of moves such as requesting that creditors' meetings be bi-monthly instead of monthly, or that a freeze be placed on the present financial position to assess possibilities for repayment. Another method is to request a three-month cooling off period to allow you to form a plan and correct the situation.

In my case, I obtained a two-year extension from the bank to pay back what I owed and after 12 months things improved. I then asked for an actual reduction in the money I owed if I could pay it before time! I received it and met the commitment.

If you have to work hard to get back on your feet, then your time is going to be limited, so arrange meetings with creditors early in the morning before you go to work. This will (a) limit the time of the meeting and (b) thin out the people who really want to push!

The second thing to do is to solve your present personal cash problem. I recall how broke we were many years ago, not knowing where our next meal was coming from; we searched behind our lounge chairs for coins and looked hungrily around for anything that could be sold to give us cash. It took many years for us to catch up on the basics of modern life, including clothes and household goods.

Never cut your living needs down to the point where you are so worried and concerned that you cannot think constructively about recovery. It may seem wise at the time to rob Peter to pay Paul, but there is always a bit more lost in the transfer than you may realise, and giving in to the demands and pressures from others automatically discriminates against the remainder of your creditors. It also does nothing for your ethical image.

In extending the deadline you should *bear in mind your own basic financial needs.* All superfluous expenditure must be axed and the minimum survival budget must be worked out and adhered to.

You will never be able to go the distance unless you reduce your cash problem. When you reduce your cash expenditure you can start to plan future moves and allocate future funds. While doing this, keep those who have been helpful informed. Your relationship with a core group of creditors must be retained and improved by communication. You will find these people will be invaluable as they help persuade the more difficult individuals to accept compromise.

As you go through the list on your countdown

sheet *try to come up with at least three ideas* of how or why it would be good to extend the deadline. Then work out a priority list, dealing with the most urgent ones first.

Clarify in your own mind and on paper the facts, because it could well be you are still being manipulated by threat rather than fact. It may be easier to extend the deadline on the more minor items and acquaint those with major interests as to what you are doing and ask them for an extension.

Whatever you do, *try and face people personally* rather than dash off a cold letter or phone call. Phone messages and letters are easy to say no to. Remember, when extending the deadline you may not solve the problem, but you have transferred it to a later date, so giving you more time to create a solution.

CRISIS CONTROLS

- Solicit helpful relationships.
- Reduce expenditure and create a survival budget.
- Extend timeframes to allow for a solution.
- Compare threats to fact.
- Personally confront your creditors.

Divide And Conquer

The last thing I am trying to do here is make it look too easy. Rather I am trying to convince you there are areas in your major crisis you can divide from the whole and solve in part.

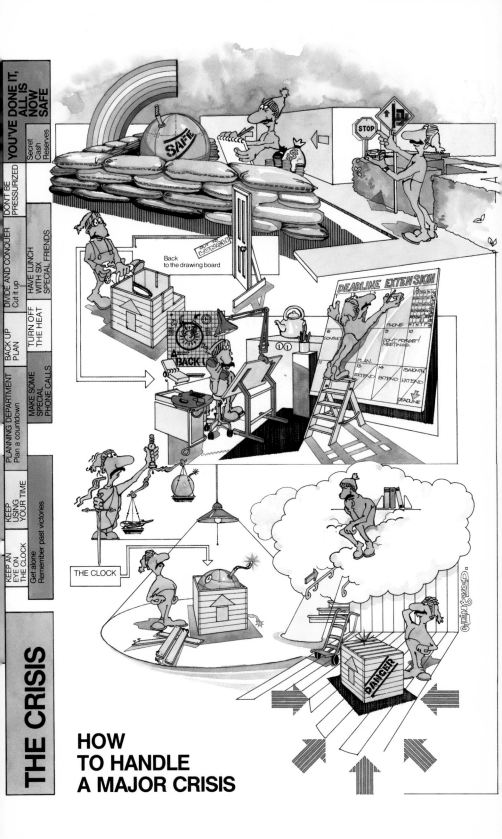

Divide And Conquer

Any military leader understands the effectiveness and strategy of 'divide and conquer'. After securing an extension in deadlines you can now concentrate your energy on one problem at a time.

Just as any machine or organisation is made up of many components, so a major crisis has many parts to the whole and *each part can be dealt with on an individual basis.* Avoid generalities and deal with specific components of the crisis; those which affect the whole and which may tip the scales in your favor.

As an example, I knew I would never be able to pay back my debts unless I was able to work on a sales commission basis, which required the use of a motor vehicle. Unfortunately my vehicle had a repossession notice out on it! My phone calls and pleas to the finance company had no effect.

Sure, this sounds like a minor problem, but in a

major crisis it was a critical factor. The car would help me become fluid and feed the family. The task before me was to divide this problem away from the major crisis and retain that all-important mobility.

Eventually I went to the finance company — without the car keys — and told them of my problem. I then spelled it out in black and white how long I thought it would take for them to sell the vehicle — and make me pay out the difference — against how long it would take for me to get a payment to them if they let me get on with the job.

I should point out here I was not one or two payments behind but rather six months in arrears, so presenting facts and figures was more productive than emotional pleas for help.

The finance company agreed and they got their first payment. I missed the next one, but caught up later and finally kept the car another two years until the major crisis was solved.

Another component of my financial strife involved a building which was on mortgage. Because I had personally guaranteed it and the payments were so far behind, the mortgagee was told to keep it. I spent time with the mortgagee and we were able to sell it at a small profit — presto another rung up the ladder.

The insurance company which held the mortgage on my house had issued a notice of sale and I was able to get two payments to them from the sale of the building — zap, the crisis was starting to shrink. Although, it was still major, I was rounding the edges off by dividing it up into components and whittling it down.

The last thing I am trying to do here is make it look too easy. Rather I am trying to convince you there are always areas in your major crisis you can divide from the whole and solve in part. You *can* reduce the size and complexity of your total crisis package.

Also remember court cases and legal battles are never as final as either side would like them to be. If you are involved in any kind of legal action it requires prime time and *consistent analytical thought* to come through. And legal wrangles always have a time factor in someone's favor. One of my big cash debts was to a legal firm which had handled an action for me and they were demanding payment of an amount which I felt exorbitant and unjustified. So I went to see them about the account.

I was told in no uncertain manner I had better pay quickly or I would be facing another legal action. I told them the amount they were asking was akin to extortion and under no circumstances would I pay.

That night at home I began to pour over old legal books and in examining solicitor and client relationships I came across an old law stating if a client was convinced a lawyer had over-charged then that amount could be taxed in the courts.

I rang the solicitor the next morning and he was surprised but happy to hear from me, thinking I was ready to pay. Imagine the shock when I said I would have the amount taxed in the courts and I was prepared to accept whatever the outcome was. He laughed and said it was an old law and I was out of order. But I persisted and told him I was determined to enforce it.

Later that day the solicitor phoned me and said if I called around at his office he had a new account, reduced by sixty per cent. Another example of divide and conquer!

I still had to press on, chipping bits off here and there, knowing full well there were still big financial problems that could take years to solve. But I did take some valuable ground and each day I edged closer to the total solution — freedom from bondage. And I was feeling encouraged all the time with each small victory.

CRISIS CONTROL
- All problems are made up of similar components.
- Dig deep for opportunities to divide and conquer.
- Each small portion you solve reduces the whole.
- Be persistent and determined.

CHAPTER SEVEN

Work On A Back-up Plan

I believe the time for us to think of the future is while the brain is working and our emotional forces are flat out.

CHAPTER SEVEN

Work On A Back-up Plan

Let's take three case histories to start off this chapter.

A friend of mine called Craig came to my office after he had sold out a large restaurant supply business. He had been enjoying himself for a couple of years, but the urge to achieve and grow was still there and he wanted to start a new business.

We discussed the possibility of a new business venture. 'What do you think I should do?' he asked.

Some time later John sat down with me. He had recently sold out his entire business and was looking for a venture that would give excitement and growth. 'Do you have any promising suggestions?' he wanted to know.

Next came William, who had just got over bankruptcy and the emotional devastation that can go along with it. What he wanted was a new job, immediate funds and an opportunity for the future.

Similar stories with different circumstances you may have heard a hundred times over. But they all were lacking in a central factor — *a back-up plan*.

As I explained to Craig, John and William, firstly, to ask someone to give you a track to run on for the future is to relinquish your God-given freedom of choice. If you relinquish that, you have *lost* your *commitment* level and are likely to fail.

I then went on to explain that during the time lapse period after a sell-out or a take-over — or even going broke — we experience a brain drain and our desperation quotient changes. We find ourselves in an entirely different environment and sometimes it becomes difficult to reason, relate and assimilate.

I believe the time for us to think of the future is while the brain is working and our emotional forces are flat out.

Sometimes it may be wise to step aside, rest, contemplate and consider after you have wound up a business. But contemplate and consider what?

A reassessment during a slow-down period after high pressure performance is often good —*but to do some planning and projections for the future while you are hot is essential.* Like Craig, John and William, you could find it difficult to come up with fresh new ideas and projects if you are out of the mainstream of commercial life. Being out of the swing it is hard to relate to new opportunities and demands.

It took years for those three men to accumulate enough information and get up a new head of steam. So it took longer to get back into the race. Each of them vowed they would never again allow themselves to let life run down without having a back-up plan.

If you know that your major crisis is going to mean the end or collapse of something in your life, then work on a back-up plan for after the event —*don't wait for the hammer to fall before you are convinced.*

While you are winding down or coming to a close, get involved in planning for future moves and prepare to change gears. If you do not, you will miss out on the momentum of being in time with the action of life.

My going broke many years ago was — believe it or not — one of the best things that happened to me. Because of necessity, I was forced to have a back-up plan for after the event *and that plan gave me the enthusiasm and energy to push forward and win.*

While it is true that a definite break between commitments will clear a lot of debris and bad memories, it may also remove your drive and divorce you from the climate that keeps the brain juices percolating.

I am told that in Chinese the word 'crisis'

embodies two actions — *danger and opportunity.* That, I believe, encapsulates the whole message. As one avenue in your life closes or changes do not let it close the door on your drive and enthusiasm to make the most out of the life God has given you.

The back-up plan is an essential part of your future, because there is a future.

Devise your plan by examining carefully what skills you have and put them down on paper in a form anyone can understand. This will create a good post-crisis atmosphere and will mean you are prepared to get the jump on the next event in your life. You are prepared for it by personal discipline, stimulation and planned timeframes.

CRISIS CONTROLS
- Don't wait until you wind down to wind up.
- Don't let your brain juices dry up.
- Plan before a change, not during a respite.
- Put your skills down on paper and get the jump on new opportunities.

Phone Six People

You will not feel so alone and you will experience the comfort and companionship of those who have gone before.

CHAPTER EIGHT

Phone Six People

I had just experienced one of the most devastating disappointments of my life. A well-established and highly respected Christian organisation with whom I had been negotiating for two years had broken its word to me.

I was shocked because I had put my professional life on the line, and I had been dropped like a hot potato. The details are not important, but my reaction to the incident is. In my state of mind at that time — feeling broken and betrayed — I knew I had to do something quick to get my spirit back on track.

I promptly prepared a hot steaming bath, lay in it and read Foxes' *Book of Martyrs*. I read of the trickery, torture and tragedy of the early Christians and how they were persecuted, even by those within the church.

I became a shouting optimist within the hour because suddenly I could relate to my current predicament and the recent events.

When you confront a major crisis what you need is *(a) perspective, (b) encouragement, (c) guidance.* And there is one way you can get all three in large measure.

Phone six people you know and respect and invite them out for coffee or a meal, without telling them why (because you need a raw response, not a prepared one). Do not discuss your own problem, but ask each of them the question: 'What was the biggest financial or business problem you ever faced and how did you handle it?'

Provoke conversation through questions to obtain more information. Do not use a tape recorder or take on-the-spot notes otherwise you will find they will place too much attention on performance; you will lose the spontaneity.

When you have gone through their problem —and their solution — relate in clear and concise terms your problem and get their response. Remember, you do not have a lien on brains and *a fresh approach will open up new and unexpected solutions.*

After the meetings, make quick extensive notes. Do it before you forget, and make particular notes on any comments or suggestions which apply to your problem. Jot down any additional thoughts triggered during the meeting.

Carry out this exercise with each appointment and write down more rather than less, because what may be uninteresting or unexciting in one context may prove to be a linchpin when related to your problems. Make sure you get a variety of positions and experiences to gain maximum diversity of input and multiple choices. Send off a note quickly to each friend after the meetings, thank them for their time and leave the door open so you can come back if necessary.

This procedure will do several things for you while handling your major crisis. *Firstly*, it will give you a huge emotional life and create energy and willpower to deal with problems. It also wil help you maintain a correct attitude. With the stories from your friends, you will no longer feel alone and you will experience the comfort and companionship of those who have gone through the mill before.

Secondly, your major crisis will be brought into perspective. You will be able to see that at least one or two of the six people will have had a crisis as bad as yours — in many cases, one worse.

Thirdly, you will realise that these people survived, and the crisis may have been a catalyst taking them on to bigger and better things. At the very least, they are the wiser for their walk through the fire.

Fourthly, and finally, the information you obtain will be something to which you can relate and will help sweep away the emotional debris you don't need.

CRISIS CONTROLS

- Select six people for a crisis 'summit.'
- Listen intently and make notes later.
- Apply the relevant information to your problem.

The Kettle Only Boils When There Is Water In It

One of the most difficult things to deal with is that during the struggle and after the crisis, time drags, seemingly forever.

The Kettle Only Boils When There Is Water In It

The title of this chapter is quite obvious, yet it seems to me that principles which are obvious are often overlooked because they are so simple.

During your crisis you are going to feel pressure from many directions. For example, if you are in a financial crisis, it is plain that everyone will want their money and they will pressure you to get it. They will persist for one reason alone —*because they believe* you will produce under pressure! But if you produce facts to show you cannot meet the debt, the pressure will fall away. However, you must be totally honest about those facts.

People will not persist in trying to obtain that which is unobtainable. It has been my experience that every problem has a limited lifespan, and over a period of time the problem either vanishes, is solved or we manage to cope with it. One of the most difficult things to deal with is that during the struggle and after the crisis, time drags, seemingly forever.

The famous Albert Einstein realised this and discovered a new dimension in time, today called the Theory of Relativity. In simple terms, *for a man sitting on a red hot stove, a minute seems like an hour, but for a man talking to a pretty girl an hour seems like a minute.*

In a major crisis, time does seem to be extended. Hours seem like days while days seem like weeks. The key is not to let your kettle boil when there is no water in it — after having done all you can, don't fret and bang at that proverbial brick wall. The reverse, of course, should apply — if you can do something to help the situation, do it and get the water into the kettle. If everything has been done, apply the biblical principle 'having done all, stand.' And that is a message you should get across to all who are pressuring you.

Another point worth bearing in mind is that *there is nothing anyone can do to break you.* They can sue you and you can survive. They can take all your worldly goods, but you are above worldly goods. They can try to manipulate your circumstances, but you can be above circumstances. In addition, they may try to control your future — which is unknown to them anyway — and they may even threaten physical assault. But you have a greater mental and physical strength, so that won't work either. In most senses, you will have to agree you are impervious and immune to everything, except yourself.

You may recall the little boy who was behaving badly and whose father instructed to sit in a chair in the corner. The youngster refused and his father spanked him until he sat down. But the last words the father heard through the sobs were, *'All right, I'll sit here 'cos you made me, but inside I'm still standing up!'*

There is another aspect to survival — dreaming. I was once asked what kept me going through three financial crises and my answer was 'my dreams'. *I firmly feel that a dream converted into a goal and committed for life is a powerful force.* It will sustain a broken and troubled period in life and dreams will guide you a long time after bad memories become forgotten memories. Success soothes all memories and we should make a point of accepting failure for what it is — a lesson learned.

We should work at maintaining composure, remain futuristic in our outlook and always resisting the shackles of the failure of the moment.

CRISIS CONTROLS
- Remember, 60 minutes equal an hour — even in a crisis.
- No one can really break or hurt you — unless you allow them.
- Dreams transformed into life goals are a personal and powerful force.*

*See P.J. Daniels *How To Reach Your Life Goals* (Tabor, 1985).

Do Not Be Side-Tracked Into Foolish Decisions

The side-track is fraught with pitfalls — it will get you into a deeper crisis which will take even longer to get out of.

Do Not Be Side-Tracked Into Foolish Decisions

Very often while under pressure and trying circumstances we allow ourselves to believe that any change is preferable to our present predicament. In this belief we are apt to make a drastic and foolish move.

I recall years ago looking at other people and really wishing I had their problems and they had mine. I found out later they felt the same — they wished they had Peter Daniels' problems! Certainly, other people's problems seem soluble while ours do not.

The reason for this is that from a distance most problems look quite simple. A closer examination shows that real complications and contradictions exist. *Because of the inward yearning for relief and* the need to put the whole sorry state behind us, we may find ourselves open to accept an idea or proposal which will side-track us.

Let me explain further. Assume you are an electrical retailer and you have fallen on hard times. Sales and profits have plunged and the creditors are at the door. Now what do you do if an attractive opportunity presents itself like a contract to buy shares in a new business with no cash outlay?

Similarly, a resale development has come up with a guaranteed result before funds are required. Just sign here, please.

Of course, it is tempting — particularly if documentation shows a proven track record. At this juncture you face three choices:

1) *Take the risk knowing and understanding the ramifications, but believing you could handle* another crisis if it eventuated.

2) *Take the risk, believing you could succeed and relieve your crisis and ignore the possibility of total loss.*

3) *Jump in with a devil-may-care attitude determined to crash through or crash. This is called going out with a big bang!*

These illustrations are not meant to be flippant; I have seen them in real life and they are as common as they are repeatable. Let me suggest that taking any of the above options will lead to a side-track. They ignore the application of clear facts and logic.

It must be realised that to become involved in sharebroking or real estate usually requires years of experience. So in those fields, or in any other with which we are unfamiliar, how can we expect to plunge with sudden insight and succeed?

Also remember that in a major crisis added pressure prejudices our thinking and it is very tempting to look for an easy way out.

It is at this point we must control our imagination and *avoid taking side-tracks which defy all good practical sense.* This book is written to get you out of your crisis and on towards success, not worsen the situation.

I have extensively lectured on this subject and know that the side-track is fraught with pitfalls — it will get you into a deeper crisis which will take even longer to get out of.

One of the most logical reasons to maintain an even keel is that your brain is attuned to the problem at hand when you are facing your crisis head on. The last thing you need is a diversion. When you shift from sound logic, you not only lose your creative energies but also your moral commitment. Furthermore, consider the damage you can do to your credibility and reputation by gambling on an outcome rather than by taking step-by-step analysis to the problem.

Do not be side-tracked by that seemingly 'perfect' opportunity unless you can demonstrate that *under all circumstances* it will not detract, subtract or side-track you from your main objective — successfully handling the major crisis and pressing on to success.

Such opportunities are indeed rare.

CRISIS CONTROLS
- Beware of schemes that promise easy solutions.
- Keep your mind on fact and logic.
- Remember you are supposed to solve the problem not side-track it.
- Keep short reins on your moral obligations.

Do Not Be Pressured Into Unwise Moves

The most obvious tactic used is to initiate a new arrangement: a counter document which you are obligated to sign or else!

Do Not Be Pressured Into Unwise Moves

The pressure and urgency of a major financial crisis produces all manner of actions and re-actions from those around you. They will either benefit or lose through your unfortunate circum-stances.

I have found the most pressing and urgent pres-sures come from direct creditors such as banks and finance companies, who are experts in cir-cumnavigating other people's crises, cutting short their losses and moving on to greener pastures.

Because financial institutions are so astute in resolving their side of a difficult situation, it is of paramount importance to review with extreme caution any move they instigate while you are under pressure.

Remember, they are entitled to be paid if funds are available — after all they loaned the money and are entitled to get it back with full interest paid. But there are certain ways they should go about it. *They should not use duress or threats.*

The most obvious tactic used is to initiate a new arrangement; a counter document which you are obligated to sign or else!

Take my word, such an arrangement *always* locks you in further and tightens the noose which could delay recovery for years.

If you are ever faced with such a situation, never agree until you at least have had an opinion from your accountant or solicitor. You will invariably finish up in a worse mess if you fall into this kind of manipulative arrangement.

I am not suggesting for one moment that you avoid or refuse to pay debts you have incurred. But what I am saying is *use wisdom and calmness in your assessment.*

By now, of course, if you are well into your major crisis, your friends and relatives will know about it and may start to demonstrate concern and involvement.

The concern for you is real and should always be taken as a form of encouragement. But be careful of their comments, advice or involvement!

Most friends and relations are more likely to offer a quick-fix answer, solutions well-intended *but devoid of any real long-term direction or* commitment.

Keep in mind there is no one but you who can feel the pain and anguish, and no one but you who will be finally responsible for the long- and short-term solutions to your crisis. Good, well-meaning friends can never appreciate the complexities and commitments of a major crisis; it simply does not directly affect them.

In a major crisis there also can be a very real danger of putting pressure directly on yourself, leading to the pursuit of an unwise, unplanned program seeking any kind of solution.

Let me suggest a simple formula for analysing a course of action.

1) Consider all the repercussions *of doing absolutely nothing about your predicament for one month*. Evaluate whether your position would improve or worsen. Be objective, even write out clearly what you honestly believe the situation would be from that perspective.

2) Note down all the advice, suggestions and threats you have received *along with your own idea of how to resolve the crisis*. Also list priorities, timeframes and energy required and examine the possibility of doing them all.

3) *After detailing (1) and (2) above get together some of those you spoke to (see Chapter Eight) and explain your plan*. In fact, launch a brainstorming session and drum up some ideas.

Now make the final decision, *even if it totally*
ignores the advice given.

CRISIS CONTROLS
- Don't sign anything in a hurry.
- Be very careful of sincere but poor advice.
- Use a formula to handle your pressures.

Go On The Attack

The key is to work at your crises continually and to attack the problems. Don't let them attack you.

CHAPTER TWELVE

Go On The Attack

Do you remember as a child lying in bed late at night when all was dark and silent. The slightest noise would send fear racing through you and you would pull the blankets over your head.

But major crises do not go away when you pull the blanket over your head! On the contrary, if ignored they can race away like a bushfire, causing more devastation.

So how do you deal with the realities of a crisis? Examining some of the great names in history —and those of today — can help.

One of the great privileges I have had in my business career has been to watch great business and political leaders in action. More particularly, to study their behavior in a crisis. *Without exception I have observed that each one went on the attack.*

General George Patton was once asked about his defence in respect to his enemy. *'To defend* you must attack' was his response.

During the credit squeeze of the sixties in Australia, Sir Bruce Small had just opened a sales campaign for real estate at Surfers Paradise in Queensland. He had to face the return of contracts and rejection by purchasers.

But he hung in there 'by the skin of his teeth' and worked his way out to make Surfers one of the most popular holiday playgrounds in the world. Sir Bruce kept working towards his goal, attacking nearly every problem front-on. He always came through stronger than before.

When building the Crystal Cathedral, Dr. Robert Schuller was confronted with rising costs, inflation building problems and limited funds. During a particularly difficult time he said: 'I would like to have a good old-fashioned heart attack and fail with dignity.' But he fought on and won the day.

W. Clement Stone, one of the world's greatest insurance salesmen, always responds to any problem with the comment — 'So we have a problem. Great. Now we have something we can get stuck into.' A lifetime of overcoming problems has proved the man right.

Paul J. Meyer of Success Motivation Institute in Waco, Texas has what is possibly the most successful business system in the world. When his son Larry was asked how dad handled a crisis, he said, 'He attacks.'

Dr. John Haggai of the Haggai Institute of

Advanced Leadership, has a unique attitude to a major crisis. He says, 'Never advertise your deficiencies.' In other words, don't run around bleating to one and all about your problems — work at them and in so doing inspire others.

During a particularly bad year I noted down what my major problems were and I'll admit they looked awesome. But during the following twelve months, I was amazed at how each one became smaller through hard work and effort. However, I found at the end of the year I had a specific set of quite new and unrelated problems!

Face facts. *We will always have major or minor crises in our lives.* The key is to work at them continually and attack the problems. Don't let them attack you.

A friend of mine has a particular way of dealing with difficult situations. He will listen intently, ask quiet but searching questions and nod his head continually, revealing little or no emotion whatsoever. He waits patiently until the end of the conversation before giving a response. He will then say, 'It seems to me we have several options here.' Then he will number off the options available. *Each option works towards a solution.*

When involved in a major crisis, don't expect it to go away, but remember that others before you have come through. Use the attack method and plot a battle plan.

CRISIS CONTROLS
- Don't hide under the blanket.
- Attack problems, don't let them attack you.
- Face facts: we will always have problems.
- Work through all the options for a solution.

So You Failed

So you failed, and now you're buried in grief,
Success has evaded you just like a thief.

But there are much gloomier horrors and more,
If you do not wake up and take count of your store.

You're alive! That's good news, and the future's
*   untouched,*
So now it is time to reflect and catch up.

Don't waste this great day with bad thoughts and
*   regrets,*
Just count off the blessings and good times you've
*   met.*

Your life can be salvaged, your ego made new,
There'll be more opportunities and choices for you.

Face up to it, friend, you're not finished yet,
Beneath all your hurts, there is still something left.

Stand erect, head held high, get ready to move,
Success has just tried you, you've something to
*   prove.*

You're made of stern stuff, much stronger than steel,
You'll win in the end, with your faith and your will!

Peter J. Daniels

NOTES

NOTES

NOTES

Keep Using Your Time

Delays and timeframes are precious jewels. Use them well to protect and propel you forward.

Keep Using Your Time

The best — and worst — component in a major crisis, next to money, is *time.*

Generally, if you have enough time you can do almost anything. By recognising the power of time, you put yourself on the winning side. And when you recognise the potential of time you are more likely to use it wisely. Do not allow waiting time to be wasting time.

You can quite often play for more time. You can accelerate time and even use idle time to create dynamic opportunities. During any major crisis, there are periods of respite or just plain times of waiting for decisions or events to unfold.

On these occasions, be alert and watch for pockets of time. Any delay in a situation can be spent in revaluation, examination and forward planning. *The usual difference between success and failure is the way in which we use or abuse time.* I have used delays in a major crisis to literally launch a lifestyle clean-up.

We are creatures of habit. You can totally change your life by changing your habits. But be careful of the half-hearted approach as it can make your future even more difficult.

When you decide to make a habit change in life you make a commitment to your subconcious mind. The subconcious will prepare to respond and give heavy assistance to that commitment —until you slip up. When you break the commit- ment — even once — you have signalled to your subconcious that you weren't serious about the change and the amount of subconcious help forthcoming is reduced.

The truth is simple: if you want total support from your inner mind, and you are serious about a habit clean-up, *make a genuine commitment and do not allow a single exception to occur.*

Use other time delays for discipline assess- ments. Go back over the last twelve months and ferret out areas of your life where you could have been more disciplined and decisive in action and commitment.

These delays and timeframes are precious jew- els. Use them well to protect and propel you for- ward. Accept and utilise the opportunities with a positive attitude and *do not waste time reliving past mistakes.*

A time break also is a good time to plan for the future. Try noting down areas of your life you are going to change. And reaffirm those principles you plan to stick by.

A renowned psychologist said many years ago that man has a 'second wind', a 'third wind', and so on. He went on to explain just when you think you have run out of puff in the race of life, you suddenly receive another 'wind'. During some delays in your major crisis you may well catch inspiration which projects you forward — if you're not dozing off!

Another good idea during a break in your time of crisis is to try and isolate yourself with trusted friends or your family. Take a week off and promise yourself you will not discuss your misfortunes during that period. *In other words, by escaping for one whole week you are going to give your body and mind some relief from the ever-present pressure and drain it has had on you.*

It need not involve expense or holiday abroad. You can spend time in such places as the city gardens, art galleries or — one of my favourite refuges — the public library (nothing like immersing yourself in good books to relieve the pressure!).

I must mention one other aspect of profound importance relevant to any respite in a crisis. This recommendation has stood the test of time of centuries and brought comfort to millions. *I am talking about the spiritual therapy of prayer.*

Not just petitioning the Almighty, but making a

thankful response for being alive, intact and still having opportunity and hope. It could be you will discover, as many have before, the missing link is faith in Jesus Christ.

CRISIS CONTROLS
- Do not allow waiting time to be wasting time.
- Have a habit clean-up.
- Escape to prayer.

Prime The Pump

Just as you cannot pump water without priming the pump, so you must have some reserves — even if only a unique idea — to get you back in to business again.

Prime The Pump

During your crisis you must not only look at survival, but also at a return to success and progress.

For you to throw out all the money left and burn up every opportunity in a futile effort to meet impossible demands is not only dishonest, it is also stupid.

It may generate a feeling of, 'Oh well, I've done all I can do,' but it will never solve the problem of paying back your creditors or getting back into business. Remember, you have an obligation to others and yourself to achieve both.

Twenty years ago I used up all my resources and afterwards realised I was sterile — I could do nothing and I still had an enormous amount of ground to pick up. The sensible thing would have been to do as much as I could without abandoning my opportunity for recovery.

You must resist at all costs the temptation to throw

everything of value at your creditors under the cloak of honesty. The really honest thing to do is give them all a chance.

By spending every cent you render yourself powerless to resolve the situation. It is true any reserves you have now will be very limited and must be protected more carefully than ever before. But do not let this situation daunt you; remember that your attitude is your greatest asset (see Chapter One).

The other thing to consider is you are now older and wiser and, in effect, success and progress will be easier second or third time around. Stories abound of those who have lost and gained fortunes many times over — they always bounce back.

What has happened to you will add to your inner resources, and you will be more aware of trouble ahead.

Just as you cannot pump water without priming the pump, so you must have some reserves — even if only a unique idea — to get you back into business again.

Now is also the time to be pragmatic, prudent and prepared to let some opportunities pass rather than make a grab in desperation at anything that comes along. I would like to suggest three principles you may find helpful in recovery. *1) Your first priority is to secure adequate living expenses,* providing the necessities of life for you and your family. But do not let this exhaust you physically. It may mean working for someone else or doing contract work — but it must give you flexibility.

It is of no use being locked into a situation where you (a) cannot use a telephone, or (b) do not have freedom to work your own hours. Maybe work early morning and late night, but secure time to get out and prime the pump.

2) *Your second objective is to find an opportunity which will serve as a launching pad.* Remember that money will always flow to good ideas; one that is practical and simple will give a good return on a minimum investment.

Many years ago while scouting around for an idea — an item in city stores, for example, that had not changed in twenty years — I came upon an old-fashioned butter warmer. It was a simple article which was filled with hot water then placed over butter making it easy to spread on a cold morning. I took it to a metal spinner and asked him to make a new sample. I obtained orders from stores for cash in seven days. (My account to the spinner was over thirty days.) The butter warmer was a novelty, but it primed the pump. Yes, simple ideas sell well.

3) *The third principle is to build permanent reserves to prevent a further crisis.* These reserves should never be mortgaged, used or speculated upon. They are the backstop to prime the pump in

the future if misfortune strikes again — *your survival kit.*

Remember business and economies go up and down like the tides of the ocean. Your reserves will almost certainly be needed.

CRISIS CONTROLS
- Reserves allow you to continue.
- The second time around is easier.
- Look for a launching pad.
- Build in reserves.

Where Did You Go Wrong?

In this life that God has given us, we become at times both our own teacher and student. The only real obstacle is ourselves and the only real diploma is a measurement we honestly put on ourselves.

CHAPTER FIFTEEN

Where Did You Go Wrong?

Time now to put pen to paper. Unless you are prepared to document your mistakes you will overlook the lessons learnt once the pressure has passed.

It is even a good idea to write a diary of day to day thoughts and events and exactly how they came about. This will bring you back to reality during the heady times ahead when you hit the jackpot.

During a five-year period when I could not put a foot right, I kept a diary that to this day is a meaningful chronicle of past experiences. Try to keep your remarks simple and do not embellish the story (you are not writing a novel!). Make it an honest, factual account of difficult times that were overcome through perseverance and diligence.

After documenting your major crisis and highlighting the areas where you went wrong, move onto a preventative plan — this is to offset future catastrophes. *You will surely face another crisis in your life, but it should not come about due to the same issues, or come without warning signals.*

Lock in a formula to prevent similar future predicaments, identifying the warning signals and subsequent steps you will take to avoid those misfortunes.

It is well worth noting at this point that if all those bad moves in the past were placed in reverse you would have ended up with a major victory instead of a major crisis! Study what has happened and you will learn something exciting from the exercise.

I appreciate that most readers of this book may not document a past crisis, preferring a mental and casual evaluation. But remember, someone once said that the only thing we learn from history is that we learn nothing from history. This is very true, because we are rarely prepared to grasp the principles of truth that work in real life situations. We hardly ever document those truths and use them as a formula for the future.

But success is more than money, it is a lifestyle of learning from mistakes, setting high goals and taking the opportunities God has provided.

By the same token, a good memory and reasoning faculties are of little use if they are not exercised and used for their intended purpose. I feel failure does build character and resilience *if it is approached with a positive mental attitude and* lessons are learnt from the past,

In a major crisis a hurtful fall may leave scars and bruising as sharp reminders. But the battle is never over and failure is never complete, just as one victory or one success is never the end. There are more challenges ahead, more disappointments to bear, and certainly more surprises in store.

However, all the time we are learning about ourselves, life in general and people and circumstances.

Always treat your crisis as a learning experience.

In this life that God has given us we become at times our own teacher and student. The only real obstacle is ourselves and the only real diploma is a measurement we honestly put on ourselves. Look at what we could have been and done against the reality of what we have done.

Many, myself included, have done far too little and wasted far too much of life.

We should push on, setting new benchmarks and new horizons of achievement for others to follow.

CRISIS CONTROLS

- Lock in a formula to prevent recurrence.
- Put your bad moves in reverse and succeed.
- Treat each crisis as a learning experience.

The Twelve Principles Of Success

May God expand your life until your destiny is fulfilled.

CHAPTER SIXTEEN

The Twelve Principles Of Success

1. Adopt a right attitude

Every successful person possesses an attitude that propels him forward. Attitude is not necessarily good or bad manners, but rather *a mind-set which takes precedence over all other principles of success.*

Attitude towards others and towards attaining the heart's desire reveals all about an individual —self-esteem, confidence and courage. Pure love, for example, cannot be fully expressed without a good attitude towards commitment. On the other hand, a fleeting and shallow love expresses a bad attitude towards a commitment in life.

A powerful attitude and response to the parade of life helps you take advantage of all opportunities and challenges.

A good attitude helps you *seek solutions rather*

than emphasize the problems.

2. Have a willingness to bear pain

I was once asked for a principle for success. My answer was the 'willingness to bear pain'. (I did not say *be* a pain!) *This is undoubtedly a secret to achievement* because success hurts at times —it often demands long nights, long days and total fatigue.

Pain also comes with criticism, pressure, failure and all those other miseries that are price tags to success.

Endure pain to the end and accept it as part of the successful person you are going to be.

3. Take control

We are totally responsible for what we do — or do not do. God made us to subdue the earth and He gave us free will with which to do it. To do this properly, we need control.

Control, in even a broader sense, means that in any situation of business or social pursuit we have the freedom to change. Therefore we are responsible to organise and guide our life. That does not mean we are behaving selfishly, but in fact behaving responsibly.

The most unselfish act you can perform is to organise your life in such a way that you are not a burden to others and to accept your life as a gift. Under this arrangement you take a hold of your own life, help others, but not follow the pack. You have control of yourself while pursuing your personal goals.

4. Give attention to detail

Attention to detail — or lack of it — very often provides a catalyst to success or failure.

We need to stop being surface scratchers and to develop habits which will enable us to find quickly that elusive spanner in the works.

We can recall situations where if only we had probed a little deeper or followed a hunch, or even given a little more care to a particular item, the outcome would have been different.

Not being a surface scratcher means looking for the obvious *and the not-so-obvious. Fill in gaps that are vulnerable in both your personal and business life. And always pay attention to the little things in life.*

5. Develop money sense

Always remember that your financial integrity in a community is a valuable asset, and your integrity is not for sale.

The fact is that today we economise to save, *but we must have an extra flow of capital to grow.* Many people major on the saving end of the scale and really rob their lives of enjoyment by overlooking the other end of the scale — money growth. Money should be double-edged. It should take care of the day-to-day needs but also cater for an increase in future needs and changing life-styles.

However, in my opinion, the most important aspect of finance is to *have a life philosophy that will prevent you becoming either a scrooge or a spendthrift.*

6. Show respect for time

When people tell me they don't have enough time, I tell them, 'You have all the time you are going to get!'

The length of your life has very little to do with the availability of daily time. The key is to respect time and get it into its real perspective. Time also is money because if you don't put in the hours, you don't get the money.

Spend a few moments considering what an hour is worth and relate its value to family life, helping others and keeping the income machine up to its full potential. Now spend a moment asking this question: 'How much would I pay myself an hour for my time if I knew I could extend it beyond my death?' *Use time wisely, program it so you do not fritter it away.* But allow yourself time to dream —that is the stuff where great ideas and plans for life come from.

7. Set purposeful goals

Goal setters are optimists because they plan

future achievement and expect to get there. Scientific studies show something mystical happens to our minds and personalities when we commit ourselves to a single cause.

As you pursue and close in on your goal it is quite amazing how things fall into place, so the outcome seems a breeze. *You may then even expand your end goal and so the process becomes self-perpetuating.*

If you don't have a goal, make finding a goal your goal!

8. Show desperation and ambition

Most people get along by going along or they keep one foot on homebase and wonder why they get left behind.

If you do not have a desperate ambition to succeed, make way for someone who has. I am not talking about ruthlessness or selfishness. I am talking about doing your best and reaching your full potential, and desperately wanting to do just that. To my mind that is an act of gratitude to God who gave you your life to use to the best of your ability. It means hard work and lots of it. It means careful thought and planning and pursuit of a goal with a passion.

Look to the Bible for those who were ambitious, but humble, for models of desperate men. Consider Paul the Apostle and John the Baptist to name but two. Even Christ's life was one of ambition and desperation.

Perform in your life with both those attributes —*and go after your goal as if your life depended upon it!*

9. Use follow through

Most lives are littered with the debris of half-finished work and unfulfilled dreams. The job has-been only half done.

Under some exceptional circumstances we cannot get the task finished. But the fact is *a great deal of failure is caused by lack of follow through.* A point worth noting is that it is far better to attempt less and complete it than take too big a bite and never finish it. I am not advocating small goals or limited dreams, but I am saying *make it a positive habit to complete what you start.* This will prevent you becoming a surface scratcher and sharpen your commitment edge.

Follow through makes a mockery of excuses, and adverse circumstances and will win more battles and reach greater successes than all those sacrificial starts and quick-fix bursts of energy. It is also a declaration of control by habit.

10. Discipline all of your life

Many times, no doubt, you have seen a father discipline a child but himself live an undisciplined life.

The disciplinarian tries and keeps on trying,

accepts personal accountability and is committed to a cause.

Discipline is essential because it flows through all areas of your life, producing moral conduct and confidence. And the discipline not to do is as strong as the discipline to do.

Discipline affects punctuality, keeping your word and the maintenance of personal habits. I consider it more than will-power. Discipline becomes a commitment to everything in life you hold good and pure.

11. Make a practice of study

In a fast-changing world ruled by the microchip and shifting economies, study is essential.

I recall a fun game held at a seminar once when I offered to buy the brains of all the participants! I could have got them cheaply because (1) *they had never trained them* (2) *they had never fed them* (3) *it was not apparent they could use them*.

Study those areas which relate to your life — finance, furniture, automobiles etc. Never have the libraries of the world held so much information, and never have they been so empty.

12. Sharpen your perception

To save energy and get down to the nitty-gritty you require perception. Without this attribute you can often go down the wrong track.

You can sharpen your perception with training.

Perception means to examine something in a deep and searching manner — and it prevents you being wise after the event. It means more than listening to words *but looking behind them.* It means looking down the road a year or two. Perception is keeping your eye on the objective as well as an eye on the means to reach it.

Courage

The gift of courage isn't rare,
It's just that it's rarely tried.
To face the future, fear or foe,
You must not ever hide.

Life is full of doubts and dents,
And knock-downs big and small.
But you, with courage as your friend,
Can rise like a bouncing ball.

Spring back and give your fears a fight,
Don't take it lying down.
Exhibit courage once again,
And gain the winner's crown.

And as you feel your strength renewed,
With vigour and with vim,
Take on a brand new fighting stance,
Erect and firm of chin.

'Come on,' you'll say to all the world,
'Deliver me your worst;
I'm ready for whatever comes —
Now who will be the first!

'I'm courage, that's my given name,
This day and ever more;
I'm here to fight until I win,
I will back down no more!'

So if you have pain that threatens you,
Or problems from within,
Great challenges or crisis points,
A bankroll that is thin.

It's courage, that's the thing you need,
To help you through each day.
A tough and ever faithful friend,
To stay with you alway.

NOTES

NOTES

NOTES

NOTES

NOTES

NOTES

NOTES